GU01017937

A Director's Guide

Effective Business Communications

HOW DIRECTORS CAN PROFIT FROM INFORMATION AND COMMUNICATION TECHNOLOGIES

Editorial Director: Tom Nash
Managing Editor: Lesley Shutte
Sub-Editor: Caroline Proud
Consultant Editor: Marc Beishon
Production Manager: Lisa Robertson
Design: Halo Design
Commercial Director: Ed Hicks
Managing Director: Andrew Main Wilson
Chairman: George Cox

Published for the Institute of Directors and BT
by Director Publications Ltd
116 Pall Mall London SW1Y 5ED
020 7766 8910
www.iod.com

© Copyright October 2002
Director Publications Ltd
A CIP record for this book is available from the British Library
ISBN 1 901580 86 5
Printed and bound in Great Britain
Price £9.95

Contents

3

Prepare for tomorrow without

creating the 'office of the future'

Prepare your organisation for tomorrow with an IP infrastructure from BT. Dependable infrastructure is vital for the future success of your organisation. And BT provide one of the most reliable solutions around – 99.69% reliable to be exact. That's why 90% of the UK's top financial institutions rely on them for their transactions. And what's more, BT build on your current technology to provide networks that meet your needs now and in the future. They'll deliver an integrated solution that is both scalable and secure. For practical ways to get your organisation moving forward, **Free*fone* 0800 800 997** or connect to **BT.com/business**

BT.com/business   **Connections that get results. BT**

Signposts for the future

George Cox, Director General, Institute of Directors

It is now half a century since computers were introduced into commercial use, so one might reasonably expect business to have mastered information and communications technology (ICT). We ought to be able to understand, apply and exploit the latest technology, routinely and without problems. But, that appears not to be the case – either in large-scale corporations, where we see so many high-profile failures, or in small companies.

The underlying problem is, of course, that technology won't stand still and that advances don't simply improve existing activities they sometimes transform the whole process.

The problem of staying abreast of developments is particularly acute for the smaller company that doesn't have the time or resources to dedicate to ICT. As a consequence, many developments that are relatively easy and inexpensive to implement are being overlooked and not exploited.

What is often lacking are clear signposts to the best ways forward. This guide is designed to help the smaller business understand many of the opportunities available today and how to make practical use of them. It contains short, definitive chapters on the core ICT technologies, including broadband, the digital office, customer relationship management (CRM) solutions, and mobile and wireless communications.

The book also covers the primary pointers to using ICT for profitable benefit, while not losing sight of the key principle of keeping business goals in mind in any change in operations.

Give your sales team an edge without a

'wilderness survival challenge'

Give your sales team the advantage of a website from BT. After all, BT gets a business up and running on the web every 5 minutes. And it's not just to sell online. It's to produce better sales leads by better managing customer information. You can see at a glance who is buying what and when. You can reach all your customers simultaneously through group email. And because the sales process becomes streamlined, your team will be freed up to chase, well, bigger game. To find out more **Free*fone*** **0800 800 997.**

BT.com/business   **Connections that get results.**

Technology as an enabler

Craig Rowland, Managing Director, Business, BT

Today's successful businesses know that work is no longer somewhere you go, but something you do. Around the clock, companies are striving to meet customer demand.

Small and medium-sized businesses, in particular, need to be able to keep pace with the new economy new and ways of working. One of the key methods is to make your business more efficient in its use and implementation of technology systems. Information and communications technology (ICT) enables businesses to drive down costs, drive up profit and be more flexible and efficient in terms of processes, people and infrastructure. Business advantage is created by using the latest technological solutions to maximise resources and turn knowledge into value.

BT has worked with world-class partners to develop simple, 'hassle-free' ICT solutions. We recognise that small and medium-sized businesses are facing greater demands and challenges than ever before. By providing straightforward, easy-to-adopt solutions, we can go some way to helping businesses meet those challenges both now and in the future.

Broadband is just one example of the way we are looking forward – it's obviously an important development for all businesses, whatever size and sector. We are fully committed to investing heavily in broadband infrastructure – having already upgraded 1,115 exchanges – and to ensuring availability through-out both rural and urban areas. Soon, Broadband Britain will be a reality for all businesses.

We hope you'll find this guide useful – it gives a thorough breakdown of the different ICT options available, including email, web access, and CRM systems, to help you get the most from your customers. It examines the key business issues for small and medium-sized business and the role that cost-effective, dynamic ICT plays in delivering solutions to these issues. Finally, it takes look at what the future might hold in terms of technological advances.

Efficient communications technology is one of the biggest drivers for business today and, we believe, the most powerful tool available to businesses striving to achieve their goals.

Chapter 1

Big ideas for small enterprises

Information and communications technology (ICT) can improve the way small and medium-sized businesses work. Jon Furmston, director, Business, BT, explains why

EXECUTIVE SUMMARY

- Falling costs have put ICT solutions within reach of the smaller business.
- Fast, reliable connections improve competitiveness – both at home and away.
- Flexible working, enabled by ICT, will transform company culture.
- A business without the right mix of technology is yesterday's business.

Small and medium-sized businesses are constantly being told to 'get on the technology bandwagon' or 'risk losing out to more ICT-savvy companies'. Today's society doesn't seem to be able to survive without email or instant access to the internet. But these forms of instantaneous communication are much more than technological crazes: they have the power to transform businesses.

As a director, with obligations to implement company strategy and realise company vision – whether as owner, manager, or as head of an ongoing enterprise – you may feel you have larger concerns than the effective running of your technology systems. You may be sick of the jargon and confusion surrounding many of today's technological devices and solutions. You may think that yet more new systems have little relevance to your business – that is, you may not see the practical benefits that they can bring.

But ICT is not just for the technically-literate: it is also for business strategists. As the next chapter will make clear, integrated and effective ICT systems can deliver direct, bottom-line benefits to the widest range of businesses – from manufacturers and retailers to specialist and niche companies.

To change perceptions and inform on a practical level, it makes sense to start by cutting through the jargon and explaining what is meant by ICT.

WHAT DOES ICT MEAN?

ICT stands for information and communications technology, that is any technology that enables information to be transferred from one point to another. This includes everything from a basic telephony system to more sophisticated office networks where voice, data, email and internet powered by broadband all combine to provide systems that truly work together to allow increased productivity and more efficient working practices. The range of solutions now available means that businesses are able to buy the mix of technology that best suits both the scale of their operations and the nature of their objectives, delivering the greatest possible short and long-term benefits.

THE DIGITAL GAP

Despite this, many small businesses in the UK have been slow to adapt fully to the latest technologies. Penetration of even basic applications such as email and internet access has yet to reach the optimum level, and only relatively small numbers of SMEs exploit e-business possibilities to best advantage and trade online.

What is stopping small businesses fully participating in the new economy? Research has identified several barriers to greater take-up and use of ICT among small and medium-sized businesses. These include:

■ *lack of technical skills and understanding;*

■ *lack of time;*

■ *lack of capital;*

- *doubts about the advantages of new technology;*

- *ignorance of the potential business benefits of ICT solutions.*

You may be familiar with these factors – some may have influenced your own decisions on ICT adoption. The question is whether, since integrated and efficient technology is now more reliable and affordable than ever before, they are still relevant.

COMPETITIVE THREATS

It is vital that the UK's small and medium-sized businesses over-come the barriers to technology adoption to allow them not only to capitalise on their position as significant contributors to the UK economy, but also to compete more effectively with businesses of a similar size in Europe and the rest of the world.

Figures show that SMEs account for 65 per cent of EU turnover. In the UK, however, small businesses collectively employ fewer people than they do in other EU countries. In addition, their productivity is lower than that of larger firms, particularly in sectors such as manufacturing.

If they are to contribute their real value to the domestic economy and to compete on a European and global stage, the UK's small businesses need to be able to work even smarter. Effective, integrated technology can propel them towards the goals of continual innovation, adaptability and flexibility, stream-lining processes, creating new business opportunities and raising the morale of staff.

BRIDGING THE GAP

So how do you know which ICT products or services, from the huge range available, are the ones to pick? What issues should you consider before you choose a supplier or a certain product? Is the most sophisticated and expensive solution the best?

For a small business short of both time and specialist staff, finding the best and most cost-effective ICT can appear the sort of challenge one would rather not confront. But the solution does not have to be complex. Simple steps, such as networking PCs so that employees can access a shared pool of knowledge and implementing a more sophisticated customer tracking system to manage key customers more effectively, can reap dividends.

As chapter 2 shows, the key to making the most of any new technology or systems is to identify the business need or issue and match the solution to it. This will mean taking into account 'legacy' systems or pre-existing arrangements where relevant. The ICT revolution does not automatically mean that you have to ditch your existing systems or write off earlier investments.

ICT solutions are not the panacea for all business ills and a good technology system will not allow a company to achieve every single one of its ambitions. This, however, is not an argument for doing nothing: ignore e-business and its associated technologies and you will create more problems than you will solve, ultimately failing to discharge your duties and responsibilities as a director.

There is a whole generation growing up that takes home internet access, email and mobile telephony for granted. Your customers both today and tomorrow will expect you to be part of this world, the new e-business world.

In particular, there are three key technological trends that will deliver business benefits:

- *flexible-working practices;*

- *broadband;*

- *convergence.*

Each of these is discussed fully in subsequent chapters.

CONCLUSION

ICT is transforming the way many businesses work, now and in the future. It is driving greater competitiveness, cutting costs and accelerating the pace of business change. Whatever the scale and ambition of your company, the message is clear: take part in the revolution or be swept aside by it.

Chapter 2

Strategic use of ICT

Technology writer Marc Beishon looks at the role of ICT in building a better, fitter, more competitive business

EXECUTIVE SUMMARY

- Deployment of ICT should be thought of as a means to an end – not an end in itself.

- The core objectives of the modern company cannot be met without modern technology.

- Many businesses are failing to exploit the capabilities of new telephony and the web.

- Broadband and convergence can increase efficiency, cut costs and improve customer service.

The use of ICT has suffered from that all-too-familiar syndrome – business planning deficiency. Systems have been put in place without a clear analysis of need and benefit. And, in the case of some dotcom boom-and-bust companies, they have been used as substitutes for sound business models. "Throw ICT at it and you'll be OK" is an approach that is doomed to failure.

Thankfully, return on investment in ICT is now much more to the fore. ICT building blocks are a key part of modern business life but their use must reflect business needs and business strategy.

BUSINESS NEEDS

Businesses face certain common issues and challenges. In the SME sector, which covers the vast bulk of UK companies, respondents to a recent BT survey said their priorities were:

1 *Maintaining positive cashflow;*

2 *Improving customer service;*

3 *Making products/services attractive to customers;*

4 *Finding new customers/increasing sales;*

5 *Creating and maintaining an effective working environment;*

6 *Reducing costs through internal efficiencies.*

Larger firms in the SME base are also concerned about recruitment and retention, while those that are more optimistic about the economic outlook are focusing more on knowledge sharing, and research and development.

Many companies also say they want to free up time for 'other things' – implying that non-core tasks are dragging them down and that they simply want to communicate better, both internally and externally.

Whatever the priority, there is a clear and important role for ICT. Maintaining a positive cashflow is underpinned by all the business processes at work in a company – and these processes are themselves underpinned by ICT building blocks such as credit management tools and accountancy software.

Improving customer service, one of the more critical aspects of retaining customers and, therefore, of generating that cashflow, is also now inextricably linked to the use of technology. Many larger companies have pioneered ICT techniques in the pursuit of better customer 'experience'. And these solutions are now available to smaller firms.

Cost reductions and internal efficiencies can be achieved by better communications – and better communications can be achieved by the use of new technologies.

SERVING BUSINESS NEEDS THROUGH ICT

There are many ICT building blocks to choose from, across a variety of technologies. But there are some obvious categories to look at in the pursuit of bottom-line returns.

Customer relationship management (CRM)

Developing the customer-facing part of the company could involve something as simple as upgrading the switchboard to allow customers to call certain staff on direct-dial telephone numbers or establishing a new group of people whose job it is to handle customer enquiries. It is almost certain to involve maximising the use of a customer database and looking at the information already available on systems such as the accounting suite.

For an increasing number of companies, it will also involve the use of email and websites. Although the vast majority of UK businesses have internet access and email, many do not use the technologies to best advantage.

A quarter of all companies employing between 11 and 500 people have no website. This is a serious omission: a company that has a web site that gives key-contact details, product-servicing information and more can fulfil the customer service aims of round-the-clock availability, convenience and reassurance.

Office communications

CRM is part of the overall communications mix within a company, which also often involves suppliers, partners and internal traffic. Often, surprisingly little attention is paid to streamlining the various communications routes in and out of the office, with many firms operating out-dated switchboard equipment that can't, for example, forward calls easily, hunt for available representatives, allow voicemail to be left (and forwarded) or help callers find people through a voice-recognition directory system.

Modern telephony can end a lot of the frustration associated with call handling, reducing pressure on switchboards and giving customers, suppliers and other external callers easier access to staff.

The office is also the focus for two very important ICT trends: broadband and convergence. After a relatively slow start in the UK, broadband is now being rolled out to great enthusiasm. It is being installed primarily to provide a fast, always-on connection to the internet, but also to be used as an effective business tool by businesses of all sizes.

It is not difficult to see why take-up rates for broadband are rapid. At a stroke, the technology allows business to harness the benefits of downloading large files much more quickly and to provide staff with a 'pipe' to the internet that can be networked.

The choice of broadband technologies – ADSL, cable, wireless and satellite – means that all businesses can potentially install a broadband channel and so gain from the ability to receive emails in 'real time' (critical for customer service), access online services such as human resources systems and have a permanent 'window' to the world wide web on every desktop PC.

The office network – the local area network in ICT parlance – can also be upgraded to a single cable carrying both data and voice. This is convergence and it has two very important benefits. First, it cuts infrastructure costs – it is far cheaper to run one network than two. (It is even possible to dispense with cables altogether with a new generation of wireless local area network technology.) Second, it opens the way for an array of new applications that contributes directly to customer service and allows collaboration among staff and external partners.

Inter-site communications

New ICT technologies are also playing a big role in helping to improve communications between offices. Again, the ability to combine voice and data has a cost benefit, while the ability to distribute smart telephony options such as voicemail around sites can improve efficiency and service.

Increasingly, companies will have the choice of linking their operations either through dedicated private cabling for converged networking or through 'virtual' networks on the public infrastructure via broadband technology.

Broadband is also a key enabler for home and satellite offices. It helps companies tackle the work-life balance issue and thereby helps solve recruitment and retention and skills-gap problems.

Remote working

It is essential to provide the increasing numbers of professionals who now work away from the office with seamless access to the same kind of services they would get at the desk.

Much of the focus for mobile applications has been on commerce – how people might buy things via their handset – but the concept of the mobile office has been taking off.

There are various stages to achieving smarter mobile working. For voice, company handsets can be integrated into the overall office calling plan and a range of divert and forwarding mechanisms used. For data, there has been a flood of applications that allows mobile access to email and to office applications, via handsets, PDAs (personal digital assistants) and notebook computers.

With the new internet-style mobile networks – GPRS and 3G – coming on stream, mobile devices will also be candidates for convergent applications that marry messaging options.

Outsourcing

One trap that many companies fall into is trying to do every ICT-related task themselves. This wastes time that could be spent running and improving the business. Broadband technology allows many core applications, such as accounting and CRM, to be hosted and run offsite. This not only saves infrastructure costs and gives automatic access to the latest software versions but also provides a ready-made way of distributing services to staff in other offices or on the road. And outsourcing isn't just for applications. You can also buy into virtual networks that provide links between offices and ask third-parties to store your data for you.

It's easy to see the attraction of the latter. Computer gurus are predicting that there will be more information created in the next two years than in the history of mankind. It's got to go somewhere; why not a secure location where disaster is unlikely to strike?

CONCLUSION

Successful deployment of ICT is about managing and facing up to change – to new customer expectations and to new competitive threats. Some 20 per cent of managing directors (and, pertinently, their FDs) already recognise an urgent need to upgrade ICT provision. That number can only grow as the pace of technological change accelerates and economic conditions get tougher.

It is an 'adapt-or-die' world. To quote Charles Darwin: "Not the strongest, not the fittest – those most responsive to change will survive".

Climb
Success
Mountain

Help people work better
without 'motivational drinkware'

There is a more reliable way to give your organisation a leg up. Speak to BT about installing a flexible working solution. The NHS did, and it's helping them significantly reduce the time their staff spend on administration. Something worth putting on a coffee cup. To find out more go to **BT.com/business** or **Free*fone* 0800 800 997.**

Connections that get results. BT

Chapter 3

The flexible friend

Technology enables employees to work more flexibly than ever before. Dave Cordy, consultant, BT Workstyle Consultancy, offers a guide to reaping the benefits

EXECUTIVE SUMMARY

■ Demand for flexible working is being driven by customers as well as employees.

■ Adoption of flexible working can increase productivity, cut overheads and help fill skills gaps.

■ Changes to working practices must be supported by a clear business strategy.

■ Homeworkers must be initiated into company culture and continue to have face-to-face contact.

Flexible working can mean different things to different people. To some, it means flexi-time, time off in lieu, shift working or annualised hours. To technology and communications companies such as BT, it means providing the ability to work anywhere and at any time – be it on the move or at home – and the freedom to fulfil working commitments at the time that best suits the individual as well as the company. It is about re-evaluating working practices in the light of new technologies and about changing practices to gain business and personal advantage.

This chapter advocates flexible working practices and offers guidelines for companies that are planning to introduce them.

WHY WORK FLEXIBLY?

We now have the technology to make flexible working possible at a level that previous generations could hardly have dreamt of. But technological progress should not be the sole motivator for flexible-work policies. The ultimate goal should be to build a better business, that benefits from higher productivity and reduced costs.

Flexible working is entirely suited to the way we live and work now. Rigid structures are anachronistic, and it is no longer feasible to rely on the nine-to-five routine. Customers expect a high level of service in the 24/7 society. There are powerful social arguments for flexible working too (see box below) and no responsible company can ignore them. Redressing the work-life imbalance could not only make staff less stressed and less unhappy but also more productive and more likely to stay with the company.

FACTS AND FIGURES

- One in eight employees works both Saturday and Sunday. (Source: DTI Essential Guide to Work-Life Balance, September 2001.)

- Almost 11 per cent of employees work 60 or more hours a week – typically in professional and managerial jobs. (Source: as above.)

- Fathers tend to be the group most likely to work long hours. Over a third (37 per cent) of men who are in full-time employment and who live with wives/partners and dependent children work 49 or more hours a week. Around one in seven are working 60 or more hours a week. (Source: Work-Life Balance 2000 Baseline Survey, Department for Education and Employment.)

- Fifty one per cent of managers feel they "don't have enough time to build relationships outside work". (Source: The Price of Success 1999, Ceridian Performance Partners/Management Today.)

- Forty one per cent of managers believe that the quality of their working life has deteriorated over the past three years. (Source: The Quality of Working Life report, published by the Institute of Management, February 2001.)

- The proportion of families with dependent children headed by a lone parent has increased over the past 30 years from less than eight per cent to around 20 per cent. (Source: Office of National Statistics, 1996.)

- Eighty per cent of mothers and 88 per cent of fathers want "more time with their families". (Source: Demos Report on Generation X, 1997.)

- The number of women in employment in the UK is at its highest ever – 12 million. (Source: The Labour Force Survey, Autumn 2000.)

WHAT ARE THE BUSINESS BENEFITS?

The benefits of flexible working are well documented and can be summarised as:

- *In the home office, employees are able to work free from interruption and can manage their time more effectively. BT has found that time with customers can increase by 38 per cent.*

- *Adaptability to changing customer and market needs.*

- *Retention/recruitment of staff – you are more likely to find and keep the best people if you offer the best working environment. Staff recruitment costs could account for as much as four times the annual salary.*

- *Frozen/reduced cost of office accommodation – property is the second highest business expense after people.*

- *Reduced commuter and business-travel costs – commuting costs in the south-east can be as much as one third of your salary, according to the* Motors to Modems *study, carried out by the RAC.*

BUILDING THE BUSINESS CASE

Like any big internal change, the switch to flexible working must be well-thought out. The key steps that a company should take are:

1. *Identify what you want to get from the initiative. For example, to reduce overheads, to get more time with clients, to increase your options for recruitment, to expand your business.*

2. *Define the objectives for the initiative and the criteria for measuring its success.*

3. *Assess the impact the change in working practices will have on all your 'stakeholders' – your customers, your suppliers, your staff – and define the potential problems as well as the benefits.*

4 *Identify your existing costs and assess how the change will affect them. This will require factoring in the following considerations:*

- *salaries and benefits;*
- *facilities/accommodation;*
- *absenteeism;*
- *productivity;*
- *recruitment and retention.*

SO WHAT ABOUT THE TECHNOLOGY?

From mobile phones to remote access to company networks and the internet, technology has given individuals new freedom not only to consider what work they want to carry out, but also where they want to do it. Companies can now get:

- *access to knowledge through online collaboration;*

- *access to information through effective communication tools;*

- *access to people through contact tools such as messaging or conferencing.*

Some key technologies that can help an organisation make the most of flexible working are:

- *Broadband – allows you high-speed, always-on access to the internet. (See chapter 6.)*

- *Mobile technology – constantly improving, this is the corner-stone of the any time, any place, anywhere approach. The introduction of GPRS cards, which plug into a laptop, allow you to access the internet or email wherever you are. Other products include the Blackberry, a hand-held device allowing always-on access to corporate email and calendar functions, and the xDA – a personal digital assistant (PDA) that gives you permanent access to the internet, email and the usual office applications such as Excel and Word, as well as being a mobile telephone.*

TEN STEPS TO SUCCESSFUL FLEXIBLE WORKING

1 Select the right people, based on sound, agreed criteria. Not everyone is suitable for flexible working. Candidates should:

- be self-motivated;
- be able to work without close supervision;
- have good time-management skills;
- be self-reliant;
- have excellent communications skills;
- have a good knowledge of PC applications used within your organisation.

2 Ensure that home workers have the right environment and can work free from interruptions.

3 Confirm that employees have maintained their dependent-care arrangements: flexible working is not a substitute for childcare.

4 Ensure that health and safety legislation requirements are covered. For people permanently based at home, a risk assessment should be made of the home-office environment, potential hazards identified and a remedial plan put in place. For the 'ad hoc' or occasional homeworker, provide guidance on safe working practices.

5 Seek the advice of your local tax office regarding the implications your flexible-working arrangements have for allowances, employee payments, or benefits in kind.

6 Consult your insurers about extending employers' liability insurance and third-party insurance cover to any home-based workers.

7 Make sure new recruits serve their time in the office – a three-month period is ideal – so they can absorb company culture and build their social networks.

8 Ensure that teleworkers are included in team meetings and have regular face-to-face reviews with their manager or team leader to maintain social contact and build team culture.

9 Maintain effective communications with the teleworkers to supplement face-to-face contact with team members, making full use of technologies such as email and audio conferencing.

10 Set clear objectives to make it easier to gauge performance. Flexible working programmes are based on trust but that does not mean there should be no appraisal system.

■   *Conferencing – allows you to replace face-to-face meetings and still have effective communications. There are voice, video and web-based solutions. It is now possible to share documents between members of the virtual office while taking part in a call.*

■   *Online collaboration – provides a secure and virtual space online, where members of a team can share information and access it to ensure documents are constantly updated.*

■   *An intranet – allows everyone in your company access to the information they need to do their job more effectively. Enables the most up-to-date information to be available for all to see, including the company directory and data on processes and procedures and performance. You can publish anything you want to share on the intranet – including notification of changes to working practices.*

Chapter 4

Ways to cut red tape

Online services can help make company admin more manageable says business journalist Peter Bartram

EXECUTIVE SUMMARY

- Red tape must be accepted as a fact of business life and then managed accordingly.
- Small businesses should review the way back-office functions work and consider replacing old technologies.
- Online services and automation save both money and time.
- There are benefits to be had across the whole admin spectrum.

Red tape is a business bete noir. And there are few signs that it is going to go away. The question for directors is how to live with it, how to manage it better. The answer lies partly in new and evolving technologies.

Paper shuffling and form filling take up too much time, companies say, and stand in the way of the real business of making money. In other words, they lead to the very thing that the management gurus counsel strenuously against: a focus on the non-value adding parts of a company.

While it will never be possible to eliminate all non-value adding jobs – administration helps keep a company running – going online can at least keep most of them in proportion.

Technology cuts down on paperwork and makes it easier to deal with time-consuming tasks such as keeping the books and finalising sales contracts. The internet, now turbo-charged by broadband connections, can save directors hours of time searching for obscure but vital information.

GETTING STARTED

Making the switch to online admin requires SMEs to make an initial commitment in both time and resources. But the longer-term potential benefits (productivity gains and cost savings) are well worth it. The way to get ahead is to look systematically at those non-value adding tasks that cause the most problems and then at ways to make them easier.

One of the most hated tasks is complying with official regulations. The government says it wants to reduce the headaches by giving companies the chance to meet more of their legal obligations, do more 'form filling', online. But so far the Government Gateway, the 'way in' to e-government services, is of limited use. It offers only six services, one of them aimed exclusively at farmers.

The two that are likely to be of most interest to small businesses are electronic VAT returns and PAYE internet services. The PAYE service allows a firm to submit a clutch of those irritating end-of-year returns – including the P35 employers' annual return, the P14 end-of-year summary and the P11D return of expenses – electronically.

The self-assessment internet service (separate from PAYE) has been beset by problems. It is possible to file returns online but the Inland Revenue's own software hasn't always worked properly.

BOOK-KEEPING

Most SMEs are likely to get the biggest online gains by looking at their whole interlocking invoicing, book-keeping, accounting and banking activity. Online book-keeping can obviate the need to employ a specialist book-keeper or accountant.

The software company Easycounting has developed an online accounting system provided through accountancy practices. So far, more than 60 practices have signed up to the service.

Instead of keeping those familiar red accounting books or installing a software package, a business signed up to the system simply logs into a secure section of its accountant's website. Then anybody authorised in the business can raise invoices and input details of purchases. Cash book entries are also logged on the site. According to Easycounting director Neil Chadwick: "The online approach takes away the need for expert knowledge of accounting or book-keeping in the business."

At regular periods agreed with the business, the accountant downloads and verifies the journal entries, then uses them to produce management accounts. The system also makes it easier to complete periodic VAT returns and end-year accounts. Chadwick reckons a typical small business could cut time spent on book-keeping by as much as 40 per cent by using such an online service.

Many SME directors do their book-keeping out of office hours, so the fact that online accounting is available round the clock is another advantage.

CREDIT MANAGEMENT

Late payment can be a serious problem for small business. A system that generates invoices easily and provides information on those that remain unpaid is part of the solution.

Some small businesses choose to use factoring or invoice discounting as a way of releasing the value of their book debt more quickly. And most of the major discounters now offer an online service. One example is HSBC Invoice Finance. In pre-online days, a company using the service would send invoices to the discounter by post, explains Peter Tandy, a manager with HSBC. The bank would input them into its system, then release a proportion of their value to the company as cash.

Now companies can send invoices direct to HSBC through an electronic link. The system speeds up the process of releasing the cash – sometimes by as much as two days. For a £1m turnover company, that means around an extra £3,000 constantly in the bank account.

There are also benefits in tracking the cash position. Users can access their own accounts instantly and see which invoices are outstanding and how much money is still due to be released. Previously, such an enquiry would have involved phone calls and, at busy times, a wait while somebody suitably qualified was found to deal with it.

It is also quicker now for a company to get credit clearance for new customers whose invoices it wants to discount. The company can input details of its new customer and receive details of credit clearance over the internet, thus avoiding a potentially laborious round of phone calls.

BUSINESS BANKING

Standing in line to pay in a handful of cheques – or get a simple account balance – while the person in front pays in bags of small change takes crucial time out of the busy director's day. Online business banking services can help end some of the frustration.

Nobody has yet found a way to pay in cheques over the internet, but it is now possible to monitor a business account online. Companies don't need to ask for statements or make phone calls – they can access account details on screen.

Unlike a printed bank statement, which will usually be two or three days old by the time it is received, on-screen statement details are right up to date. Moreover, if a company has more than one account, it is possible to move cash between them electronically. Again, being able to deal with a bank 24 hours a day is a benefit for busy directors. When Co-operative Bank first opened its online business banking service, it was amazed by the number of people who accessed it in the wee small hours.

SUPPLY CHAIN MANAGEMENT

Two online activities that have taken off among corporates are e-sourcing – finding and concluding deals with suppliers – and e-procurement, managing a continuing flow of purchasing activity. So far, SMEs have been slow to adopt these, partly because they are more complex to manage and more costly than some of the other online services. Things, however, are now changing.

"There's no reason why smaller companies shouldn't get the efficiency savings that e-sourcing is all about," says Helen Mannion, the e-practice development officer at the Chartered Institute of Purchasing and Supply. Mannion points out that the driving force behind e-sourcing is reducing costs.

Some e-sourcing consultancies base their charges – for conducting activities such as online auctions, for instance – on a proportion of the savings. So, in the right circumstances, e-sourcing needn't cost anything.

Companies such as FreeMarkets, which has a useful e-sourcing learning centre on its website, and e-Breviate are among the leading consultancies. But if an SME wants to dip its toe in the water, a useful first stop is www.yell.com, a simple way to source suppliers electronically.

E-procurement, Mannion points out, is able to cover everything from raising a requisition to payment of the invoice. At the simplest level, email is used to deal with suppliers. Those companies that want to develop a more sophisticated e-procurement system often turn to specialist companies such as AmmNet.

PERSONNEL MANAGEMENT

SMEs invariably have less sophisticated human resources functions than the corporates, but they have to comply with a similar volume of legislation on employee rights. (Witness the requirement for any company employing five or more staff to nominate a pension scheme.) Websites such as www.hrzone.co.uk and www.hrmguide.co.uk provide briefing material on legislation as well as many other topics.

Angela Baron, an adviser at the Chartered Institute of Personnel and Development, believes SMEs should look at three key online areas for efficiency improvements. These are:

- *Recruitment. As many as 75 per cent of vacancies are now advertised online – either on third-party websites or the recruiters' own. More companies are prepared to accept emailed CVs and to issue application forms electronically.*

- *Day-to-day human resources administration. Many corporates have adopted a 'self-service' approach whereby it is encumbent upon employees to update their own personnel files when, for example, they move house or undertake a training course. Such a system may be particularly useful for SMEs that have a dispersed or peripatetic workforce that is difficult to monitor.*

- *E-learning. SMEs often find it difficult to spare the time and the money to send key staff on courses. Allowing them to undertake courses online – partly in their own time – ensures vital workplace hours are not lost and keeps costs down.*

CONCLUSION

Companies that want to release themselves from the downward spiral of more and more admin work leading to less and less productive business time have to develop a realistic plan for change, with technology at its centre. Those that do will not see red tape disappear but they will discover ways to cut some of it back to size.

KEY STEPS

- Assess which areas of admin cause most trouble and review online services that could make them easier to manage.

- Make a realistic assessment of the cost and time savings by moving online – ask others for their experience.

- Prioritise services to go online – do not try to change too many different things at the same time.

Chapter 5

Prepared for all emergencies?

Business continuity plans are designed to keep ICT systems going. But what should they include? Technology writer Nick Langley investigates

EXECUTIVE SUMMARY

■ Directors have a legal duty to minimise the risks associated with ICT failure.

■ Business continuity plans should cover prevention and mitigation – not just disaster recovery.

■ The cost of a solution should not be bigger than the size of the risk.

■ Plans should be communicated to employees and other stakeholders.

An iconic photograph from the blitz shows a milkman carrying his crate across a field of rubble, while tin-helmeted firemen struggle with a hose behind him. The message is clear: it's business as usual.

Britain's businesses have been disrupted by bombs since then, notably in Bishopsgate at the edge of London's financial district in 1993, and in the heart of Manchester's retail district in 1996. Whether or not they carried on as usual depended, in part at least, on the quality of their business continuity or disaster recovery planning.

THE IMPORTANCE OF BCM

Business continuity management (BCM) has at is heart the rapid recovery of 'lost' business-critical ICT systems. It is not, however, just a job for the IT department. The 1999 Turnbull report on corporate governance, with its emphasis on risk management, effectively turned it into a boardroom issue. "Executive management," said Turnbull, "is responsible for managing risks through maintaining an effective system of internal control, and the board as a whole is responsible for reporting on it."

Business continuity is a central issue, then, for every organisation. At its best, BCM is more than just an insurance policy that becomes 'live' in the 'unlikely event of an accident'. It is about company culture and ethos. It is about commitment to best practice. And it is about being pro-active rather than reactive.

Bharat Thakrar, a senior consultant with BT, defines BCM as:

- *Providing customers/citizens with services they want, when they want them, regardless of external issues.*

- *Maintaining corporate image and protecting both tangible and intangible assets – 'while you can insure against material loss, the damage to goodwill and your brand could be irrecoverable.'*

- *Developing a risk-based approach across the organisation; embedding risk analysis into existing processes.*

The scope of business continuity plans has widened to include the supply chain. Do the suppliers on whom you depend have their own contingency plans? Do you have a reliable second source?

"The discipline of BCM includes not just IT issues, but all risks that could adversely affect the interests of your organisation's stakeholders – from shareholders to employees and suppliers to customers," says Thakrar.

FORMING A STRATEGY

Despite its importance, BCM is somewhat neglected by British business. The Chartered Management Institute says only 36 per cent of private listed companies have a business continuity plan (BCP), and 17 per cent of UK organisations with 1,001 to 5,000 employees have made no preparations to deal with business disruption.

So how do you start to form a BCP and what principles should you bear in mind?

When preparing his report, Nigel Turnbull, chairman of The Institute of Chartered Accountants Internal Control Working Party, said: "Dealing with serious risks and their effects...should not be at the expense of the company profitability and operational function." Key points are:

■ *Keep a sense of proportion and formulate policies that are in line with the company's profile and objectives.*

■ *Tailor plans to what's needed to maintain business as usual, within budgetary and practical constraints.*

■ *Ensure plans reflect the IT-dependency of the business. (This varies by sector rather than size: business victims of the Manchester bombing included both Royal & SunAlliance and the poetry publisher Carcanet.)*

■ *As a first step, undertake a thorough analysis of potential risk, and determine whether solutions will be cost-effective. (A financial institution may have every one of its transactions 'backed up' on computers at a geographically distant site that is ready to take over the minute disaster strikes the main facility but not even the richest business can afford to pay a duplicate team of staff to play cards and drink tea until the call to action comes.)*

■ *Question whether you can afford to protect yourself from a specific risk when the plan is being put together. This is particularly important for smaller companies.*

■ *If the solutions involve changes to working procedures, or an additional burden on staff, make sure these are factored in at the planning stage.*

REMEMBERING THE BASICS

The most everyday technologies can be some of the most business-critical. And this fact is sadly sometimes overlooked. A recent Chartered Management Institute report found that while 69 per cent of companies had protected their IT capability, fewer than five per cent had made contingency arrangements for their voice telephone systems. Because voice communication is so ubiquitous and cheap, it's easy to assume that it will be quickly and easily replaced. But most telecoms maintenance contracts don't cover disasters, and installing a new private exchange, new lines and internal cabling could take weeks - possibly longer if many customers have been affected.

Making full use of communications networks, including the internet, can itself be one of the cornerstones of business continuity planning. Get your organisation used to communicating via the channels that will not close down in the event, say, of terrorist attacks/campaigns. In the aftermath of the World Trade Centre bombing, Forrester Research principal analyst Carl Howe advised that for the foreseeable future, the best way to conduct business is electronically. "Videoconferencing can help provide face-to-face contact, while email, instant messaging and faxes can handle much of the necessary communication. For companies that currently do not use Webcasting technologies to communicate presentations to customers and partners, now is a good time to start."

PREVENTION AND MITIGATION

Clearly, BCM plans should cover not just recovery, but also prevention. "Prevention rather than crisis management is the key to success or failure," says John Sharp of the Business Continuity Institute. "Continuity plans help prevent disasters."

When prevention is impossible there should at least be mitigation. "There are certain risks that can be prevented altogether, for example, you can maintain up-to-date virus protection software on all your systems," says Thakrar. "Next is a class of risks that you can't prevent, but you can mitigate the effects of. Two examples of mitigation strategies are multi-skilling so that essential skills do not reside only in one or two individuals and home-working to reduce dependency on one or two key sites."

Staff-related risks are often forgotten. In February, the Chartered Management Institute published the results of a survey sent to 674 of its members. Among its conclusions was that "IT failure is much planned for, and loss of skills a great deal less so, yet it is loss of skills that are perceived as having the greater potential impact on organisational costs and revenues".

NETWORK SECURITY RISKS

It is not just loss of skills that is a problem. Sometimes, companies are at risk from those who continue to work for them. A recent report by analysts IDC warned: "Spending cuts are putting employees under more pressure, and, as a result, careless employees, malicious ex-staff and security breaches are becoming the most frequent causes of business downtime within telecommunications companies." This is a conclusion that could equally apply to other businesses. In fact, research indicates that employees and insiders account for 70 per cent of all attacks on computer networks, and that risk increases in line with increases in the number of people with access to the network.

"As corporate networks open up to ever more users and the business role of the internet expands, it is inevitable that companies will face a greater threat from cyber crime, hacking, viruses and major systems breakdowns," says Stuart Horwood, managing director of BT Wholesale Markets.

So a business continuity plan needs to include network safeguards that face inwards, as well as protections such as 'firewalls' that guard against malicious penetration from outside. Among the services and products available is online vulnerability assessment, which uses scanners to identify weaknesses on networks and computers before they can be discovered by hackers.

Other network monitoring tools can detect suspicious transactions, or unusual patterns of activity, inside and outside the organisation. Some of these can spot inappropriate internet use – helpful in preventing staff 'cyber-skiving' and also in protecting the company from the embarrassment (and potential legal costs) of offensive material getting on to the network.

As a barest minimum, every organisation needs to protect access to data by internal staff, using passwords and user names and levels of authorisation.

THE CASE FOR BCM

- Your customers expect continuity of supply in all circumstances.

- Your shareholders expect management to be fully in control, and to be seen to be in control, of any crisis.

- Your employees and your suppliers expect you to protect their livelihoods.

- Your company's reputation and brand need to be safeguarded.

- It is implicit in good corporate governance and demonstrates best practice in business management.

Source: The Business Continuity Institute

COMMUNICATING THE STRATEGY

No matter how comprehensive your business continuity plan is, it needs to be communicated both inside and outside the company. The Chartered Management Institute's survey revealed that not all businesses understood this – and that they could suffer because of it. "It is somewhat disturbing that over a third of organisations who have a BCP do not communicate it to their staff. It is also of concern that there is poor communication to suppliers and customers. This year's survey reveals that it is customers and potential customers who are acting as a catalyst to change organisations' approach to BCM. Thus, customers are asking for BCM, but organisations are failing to communicate their BCPs to them."

Chapter 6

Broadband's big leap

Broadband technologies mean more speed and more capacity. Ian Bushby, broadband marketing manager, Business, BT, explains why

EXECUTIVE SUMMARY

- Broadband turbocharges the information superhighway, cutting waiting and downloading times.

- It offers a permanent connection to the net and could eliminate the need for a second line.

- Broadband cuts down waiting time on the internet, helps to improve efficiency and increases productivity within a business.

- New satellite options should bring broadband to more remote and rural areas.

The term 'broadband' has come to be a generic label for a set of technologies that offers more bandwidth, more capacity, than previously available for a realistic cost. At its most basic, broadband makes the internet a more satisfying experience: it means less waiting and better web 'service'. It can be up to 10 times faster than a normal telephone line and provides an always-on, robust connection.

Initial costs meant that broadband had a relatively slow roll-out in the UK. But, as prices have fallen, take-up has rapidly increased.

There are a number of ways that broadband technology can be introduced into your business: via telephone line, cable, wireless or satellite. What follows is a summary of the benefits and limitations of each of these technologies, respectively.

ADSL
Features

ADSL, from BT and its partners, is the most widely deployed broadband technology in the UK and is now available to more than 60 per cent of businesses. It allows:

- *Faster speed – ordinary telephone lines are transformed into high-speed digital channels capable of carrying data at a much higher rate than achieved with a normal telephone line. Files can be downloaded at much greater speeds. Email and web services are far faster than they are through dial-up modems or the Integrated Services Digital Network (ISDN).*

- *Simultaneous telephone usage – you can make and receive telephone calls while using email and the internet.*

- *'Always on'/permanent connection – users can access email and online services and applications immediately, without the hassle of having to establish a dial-up connection first.*

- *Flat-rate tariff – customers pay a monthly subscription fee but do not pay any call costs for the time that is spent online. Thus, internet costs become controllable and predictable.*

- *Connectivity – multi-user products give you the ability to connect your workforce for data sharing and collaboration.*

Business benefits

The ability to use the internet more quickly and efficiently than before has clear productivity benefits. Even if your staff only use the net for homeworking or simple research, sitting around waiting for web pages can waste a lot of business time. With ADSL, a lot of that waiting goes: efficiency is increased; project turnaround times improved.

The technology allows you to download content-rich material, such as video, presentations and music in a short space of time. It also provides the bandwidth for applications to be run more efficiently. Accounts, financial systems and databases can be accessed and updated remotely.

CASE STUDY: PAL INTERNATIONAL

Pal International, a family-run business based in Oadby near Leicester, approached BT to install broadband into its offices last year. Chairman, Richard Brucciani, explains why: "We needed the technology to increase efficiency and reduce costs. We now save about £7,000 a year on the costs of lines, so we're paying less for a much better connection."

Pal International has 110 employees, of which a third are based outside the UK in Singapore and Europe. The company manufactures hygiene workwear and disinfectant wipes for the food service and food processing industries and for the healthcare sector.

For Pal International, speed is not the only advantage of broadband. The technology acts as an enabler to the business, allowing it to put into practice more streamlined procedures and directly improve customer relations. The company uses a specialist customer relationship management system that is run across all 35 of its networked computers and linked to the telephone system. The CRM software runs more efficiently due to the always-on broadband connection; orders can be processed more quickly and customer records can be constantly updated.

Apart from initial teething troubles when the technology was first installed, the BT connection has been totally reliable, which has enabled IT manager Lee Dilkes to spend less time on short-term trouble-shooting and more time on long-term and pro-active IT projects that will benefit the company.

Brucciani is very positive about the future. There are plans both to open a warehousing operation in Shanghai to further develop the company's Far Eastern markets and to increase share of export trade with European and Middle Eastern markets. The use of technology is an intrinsic part of the planning process. One idea is to connect up the rest of the group with broadband to allow real-time videoconferences between the Leicester and Singapore offices.

Brucciani concludes: "The broadband technology really has had a huge impact on our business, saving time and money and helping to drive efficiency and improve customer service. The company couldn't function in the same way now without it."

The potential cost savings for your business are significant. If you are connected for more than just a couple of hours a day you probably won't be paying much more than you would in call charges from previous dial-up methods. With both the analogue

PSTN (Public Switched Telephone Network) system and ISDN, many businesses have to have a second line installed so that they can receive voice calls while being connected to the net. ADSL can reduce the need for a second line – an obvious cost saving.

CABLE, WIRELESS AND SATELLITE

The next most widely deployed broadband option is cable, from operators NTL and Telewest. The services provided are very similar to ADSL, but delivery is via the same networks used for TV services. The technology is being heavily promoted to residential users. Generally, though, if you cannot get cable TV you cannot get broadband cable. Even some city areas are excluded.

Various companies, including BT, are also now offering wireless broadband services. Transmitted from ground stations, these services are available mainly in urban areas.

For those outside the main conurbations, broadband beamed to and from orbiting satellites could be the answer. Satellite brings broadband technology to remote areas.

CONCLUSION

The technology continues to progress. Already companies are trialling new variants of DSL, such as SDSL (the 's' stands for symmetric) in the London region. This will enable businesses to take advantage of high bandwidth speed and capacity in both directions, sending and receiving data at the same time. This is likely to appeal to businesses who are heavy data users.

Broadband unlocks the huge potential of the internet. It is the technology we have been waiting for. As new products come on to the market, availability increases – and competition intensifies.

Chapter 7

Building a digital business

The 'office of the future' is now available in kit form from one-stop shops. Technology writer Marc Beishon looks at digital packages

EXECUTIVE SUMMARY

■ Exploiting new, digital technologies is an imperative not an option.

■ The digital office is not beyond the means – or the capabilities – of the SME.

■ Packaged solutions can offer good value for money and end maintenance worries.

■ 'Package deals' are now available from telecommunications companies.

The term 'digital office' is open to interpretation. Suppliers of printer, scanning and networking technologies have used it in the same breath as the much-vaunted – and probably ever-mythical – 'paperless office'. But it is about more than the streamlining of document production among groups of users. It is about the streamlining of ICT technologies.

Since the rise of the internet, the digital office has become part of the overall e-business picture, with the ability to integrate email and web-style applications across networks, both internally and externally.

Essentially, internet communications technology is converging with office systems – and the result is that companies need to equip themselves with ICT that can exploit, for instance, seamless integration between employee desktop PCs and a website that is hosted remotely (see case study).

OPTIONS FOR THE SMALL COMPANY

Many small and medium-sized enterprises have been on the side-lines of this 'e-revolution' (see chapter 2). But joining in does not mean huge capital outlay or the hiring of an expensive, dedicated IT manager. Third-party specialists and suppliers can effectively deliver the digital office to your door.

WHAT DOES THE DIGITAL OFFICE LOOK LIKE?

Basic features of the digital office include:

■ *PCs or Macintoshes running web browsers and email applications.*

■ *Digital lines – with broadband technologies such as ADSL offering high-speed internet access.*

■ *Printers – inkjets or lasers; sometimes networked, sometimes not.*

■ *A website carrying company contact details, product information etc.*

■ *An intranet that publishes and provides easy access to important company information.*

HOW DO I GET IT?

A few years ago, assembling a digital office solution would have been a hard task: several suppliers would have had to be called in. It would also have been expensive: low-cost broadband internet technology was unavailable.

Now, the digital office comes in packaged, almost 'out-of-the-box' form. Companies such as BT bring together top brands such as Cisco, Dell, Microsoft and Nortel in reasonably-priced packages.

These 'digital package deals' are designed to take the hassle out of buying ICT and to suit the specific needs of businesses. They can include support and maintenance as well as installation. There are also flexible payment options to help companies to spread the costs.

It is possible to customise the package to suit individual needs. Options can include:

- *Single-user solutions – these provide everything a business needs to access the internet via a single PC connection.*

- *Multi-user solutions – when companies outgrow their single PC dial-up connections, they can now install a local area network (LAN) that links together all the PCs and peripheral equipment to optimise their use of technology.*

- *Wireless LAN service – this is aimed at companies that would benefit from a local area network, but do not want the constraints of cabling. The 'target market' includes businesses that occupy properties unsuitable for traditional LAN installations, such as listed buildings, and businesses that plan to move premises regularly.*

- *PC adoption – even if a business has its own PCs, it can hand over the responsibility for support and maintenance and get remote help-desk services.*

DO I NEED A DIGITAL OFFICE?

The arguments for the packaged route include:

- *Low maintenance: since the solutions are designed to be simple, you do not need a high level of IT skills to manage them. In theory at least, you get the latest technologies without the need for an ICT specialist on site. Some training is provided after installation and dedicated help desks can deal with subsequent problems.*

- *Streamlining: because the technologies come as part of an integrated package they are likely to work well together.*

- *Time savings: streamlining can result in faster business processes. Technologies such as broadband can cut internet waiting times (see previous chapter).*

- *Cost savings: saving time saves money, improving productivity and efficiency. Paying one bill for one package of products and services allows you to keep track of and plan for technology costs as you grow. The package deal is likely to be cheaper than going to separate suppliers for constituent parts and requires no up-front capital outlay.*

CASE STUDY: TRB

TRB, a subsidiary of Japanese company Tokai Rika, specialises in the manufacture of electrical car components and supplies BMW, Saab, Toyota, Opel and Volvo. It was set up early in 2000, has around 100 employees and is based in North Wales

TRB's MIS engineer, Phil Riley, ordered BT's Digital Office Work Smarter package in 2001. The package was developed for companies that have already embraced the internet and are enjoying fast growth. It includes 'always-on', broadband-enabled connectivity to the internet, web hosting and ASP virus scanning.

TRB's main priority is a reliable system. Most of its key customers place their orders on secure web pages, which are then accessed by employees. It used to take 20 minutes to download order details. Download times have now been cut to just over two minutes. Riley estimates this saves the company at least eight hours a week, around 416 hours a year.

Virus scanning has saved Riley around half a day a week. Before the package was installed, he had to deal with viruses and problems of infected e-mails manually. He comments: "The system allows me to better allocate my time to projects that will improve the way the company will work."

In terms of other returns on the initial investment, TRB makes a saving of £200 a quarter on its call charges. This is mainly because employees working overseas can dial in to the network at local-call rates.

TRB's next project is the development of a company intranet. It will be run on the company's own servers and designed, updated and managed in-house, eliminating the expense of an external designer and host.

The intranet will run applications such as expense reports, facility booking systems, calendars, discussion forums and personal profiles. Employees will be able to access it wherever they are and update details of their movements and work in real time. This will streamline internal systems, resulting in greater productivity and better customer service.

- *Stress free: takes the hassle out of buying ICT solutions from several different providers at unknown cost.*

ARE THERE ANY CAVEATS?

Broadband is not available to every business/home office in the UK (see previous chapter). For some digital office purposes, however, ISDN lines can be suitable.

There are training issues surrounding the switch to full-blown digital. A 'tutorial' by the supplier won't be sufficient. As you grow and recruit new members of staff – or just replace old ones – there will be a need for more training. There might also be cultural obstacles: people working in traditional offices are used to handling and filing paper, and may find it hard to come terms with concepts such as intranets and remote websites.

As with all technology installations, the business goals must come first. Don't expect a digital office package to transform your business unless you've addressed the processes it can improve.

Work together anywhere
without 'off-site meetings'

A more convenient way to hold meetings is with BT's Flexible Working Solutions. Thanks to BT's Conferencing Service, Acadamee Consultants have significantly improved how they hold meetings, cutting hotel and travel costs by £82,000 a year. And ketchup stained cuffs are no longer an issue. To find out more go to **BT.com/business** or **Free*fone* 0800 800 997.**

Connections that get results. BT

Chapter 8

The case for outsourcing

As more specialist providers enter the market, outsourcing, says technology writer Nick Langley, is coming of age

EXECUTIVE SUMMARY

- Companies are increasingly turning to multiple external providers to serve their ICT needs.

- Network security and data warehousing are among the services now 'out-tasked'.

- Out-tasking can cut overheads, increase efficiency and plug skills gaps.

- Companies must not be passive partners in outsourcing deals: make the contract work for you

Outsourcing has come a long way since the early 1990s, when organisations handed over their IT functions wholesale to services companies whose value propositions were based on crude percentage savings on current expenditure.

The Oxford Institute of Information Management says that while big, single deals can cut costs, it is often at the expense of flexibility of IT operations and business strategy. Outsourcing should not just be about reducing costs. It should be about greater business effectiveness, understanding your cost base and measuring how IT investment affects overall levels of revenue.

THE NEW MODEL

As big outsourcing deals fell from favour, companies turned instead to multiple deals with companies specialising in particular tasks – such as network and storage management, Virtual Private Network (VPN) provision, security, voice and data integration, and web hosting. A recent survey by IT consultants Cutter Consortium found that 73 per cent of IT professionals believe the benefits of working with multiple outsourcing vendors outweigh those of using a single outsourcing provider.

THE BUSINESS BENEFITS

Outsourcing takes advantage of the economies of scale the vendors enjoy. Customers can cut their investment in equipment, infrastructure, software, staff and management. (According to the Outsourcing Institute, shortage of skilled staff is the number one reason for outsourcing.) Outsourcing also provides a safeguard against obsolescence: it becomes the supplier's responsibility to keep equipment and skills up-to-date.

Early in 2002, IT researchers RS Consulting interviewed 424 IT decision-makers from six European countries. Among companies that outsourced their hosting requirements, there was an average cost saving of 30 per cent. The companies also cited benefits such as improved business efficiency (40 per cent), reduced headcount (27 per cent) and higher customer satisfaction (14 per cent).

THE NEW SERVICE PROVIDERS

Traditional outsourcing companies, such as EDS and IBM Global Services, have been joined by businesses that are well-established in other industries and by newcomers such as telehousing specialists. Telehousing, or co-location, involves customers handing over telecoms and IT equipment to a third party, which manages them at one or more secure locations.. Thanks to the recent downturn in telecoms, there is plenty of telehousing accommodation available, and prices are competitive.

SECURITY SERVICES

According to IT research and consultancy providers Yankee Group, 12 per cent of SMEs plan to outsource security services in 2002. "They continue to be challenged to spend the money to acquire security technologies, and at the same time to hire and retain the level of security expertise to support their systems," says the group.

MYTRAVEL

The online travel agency MyTravel believes outsourcing meets its business objectives

"Our business plan was to sell our services through a centralised web portal, with the aim of increasing our overall sales revenues, while reducing our distribution and operating costs," explains Stephen Lightbody, senior technical consultant.

"Once we conducted a cost/benefit analysis comparing in-house management to a third-party provider, we realised it was not feasible to manage the development of communications links between our centres or develop a server farm internally. Outsourcing not only reduced the business and technology risk involved in this project, but also saved us a considerable amount of money."

Richard Matlus, research director for the IT specialists Gartner, agrees that using an external service provider (ESP) provides a better return on investment. "Most have already invested in sufficient security measures and have business continuity plans in place," he says.

Security also needs to cover the extended corporate network, which includes remote and mobile employees, suppliers and customers. For this, companies are increasingly turning to Virtual Private Networks, supplied and managed by specialist third parties. VPNs provide both secure connections and the opportunity to manage access by decentralised users in accordance with the organisation's policies for internal users.

STORAGE SERVICES

Outsourcing vendors are beginning to offer storage management services. Graham Titterington, senior analyst at IT consultancy Ovum, says storage requirements are doubling every year. "Companies want to expand storage in a more controlled manner and, because of the current economic climate, they are focusing on capital financing considerations. Add in disaster recovery and the need to secure sensitive corporate data, and suddenly outsourcing storage management becomes immensely attractive."

GUIDE TO GOOD OUTSOURCING

- Both partners should have access to all relevant financial information. 'Open book accounting' is essential if costs and benefits are to be shared.

- The contract needs to take account of future business changes and how the costs will be shared.

- Make sure the team you meet in negotiations is the team you get once you've signed the deal.

- Make sure the contract has an exit strategy, making clear who pays for what if the relationship breaks down.

- Don't get locked into an outsourcing relationship. Ensure your contract gives you the right to obtain the information a new bidder will need.

- Don't expect too much from your supplier. Customers have responsibilities, too.

The data may continue to be stored at the customer's site, where there's no dispute about ownership if the service provider goes bust – as a number of storage service providers (SSPs) set up on the back of the dotcom boom, have done. On the other hand, backup and business continuity require geographical separation, which remote network-based services can offer.

With their economies of scale, SSPs can provide round-the-clock management and availability – something that might be beyond a company's in-house IT team. Because they buy in bulk, SSPs claim they can cut costs to users by as much as 30 per cent.

Traditional outsourcing vendors provide storage outsourcing services, but they are being joined by telecoms companies. "Telcos are massive users of storage for their own data and have the facilities and internal expertise," says Titterington. "They can enter at the low end with low overheads, which will appeal to small to medium enterprises. Data storage is a key issue for SMEs, but since it's so expensive to build and manage their own solutions, outsourcing is the most viable answer. It could also provide SMEs with affordable business continuity solutions."

THE CAVEATS

Outsourcing arrangements are only as good as outsourcing contracts. A big outsourcing agreement can take a year to put together. Smaller 'out-tasking' contracts are less complex, but still need close attention.

The uninitiated can be caught out. Suppliers have been cheerfully pocketing the difference between what the customer agrees in advance to pay for hardware and software and the actual cost, which has been falling sharply in recent years. Last year, the House of Commons Public Accounts Committee (PAC) demanded EDS share more of the savings it was making on hardware in its contract with the Inland Revenue.

Chapter 9

No hang-ups about call handling?

Call centres are not the only way to make customer-call handling more efficient. Marc Beishon, business and technology writer, looks at options for the smaller firm

EXECUTIVE SUMMARY

- Audits of incoming calls can highlight areas for improvement.

- New, voice-activated technologies can relieve pressure on switchboards.

- Modern equipment is the only way to deliver modern service levels; outsourcing may be the way to get it.

- Most up-selling and cross-selling opportunities still arise during phone conversations with skilled agents.

When it comes to the business of taking telephone calls, it is the big, formal call centres that (often for the wrong reasons) get the attention. These centres usually have an impressive array of technology – 'popping up' customer details on screen while a call is in progress, passing calls to available agents and, increasingly, integrating other customer traffic such as email and website communications. But they do not have a monopoly on technology. These days, there is no reason why even relatively small companies shouldn't have access to similar techniques.

Beyond the formal, dedicated customer service and telesales centres, are several thousand 'informal' operations where taking and making calls is an integral part, rather than an all-consuming whole, of people's jobs. And beyond these relatively unstructured groups, are many more departments within companies where there are distinct patterns of call activity. To improve call handling, then, several steps can be taken:

- *Analysis of call patterns to reveal problems and opportunities.*

- *Upgrading/replacement of equipment to enable better call-handing facilities.*

- *Outsourcing of technology or particular call services to a dedicated agency.*

- *Use of freephone or local-rate numbers.*

- *Convergence of voice and data systems.*

ANALYSIS

The study of call patterns is probably not a job for a company to attempt on its own. A consultant could be put on the case, and the company switchboard could yield some useful management reports.

Alternatively, you could get technological help. An option from BT, network call performance, allows up to 50 lines to be monitored and a number of reports generated. At the most basic level, you get data on incoming calls, showing those received and those that were attempted, as well as the most commonly dialled numbers from a site. Digging deeper, more detailed reports reveal the split between incoming and outgoing calls at any site, the time taken to answer calls, and the frequency and duration of outbound calls. All the data can be downloaded to a spreadsheet.

Acting on the data could mean a radical change – setting up a group for a new customer-facing business process – or just streamlining existing communications. If an internal group is making lots of outbound calls at a certain time of day, say on routine account management activities, it could mean that there is an opportunity to get feedback on service, or to target certain customers for up-selling or cross-selling. If customers are calling several branch offices with service-related enquiries, routing the calls to a central resource could help free people up.

THE JOHN BANKS GROUP

The John Banks Group, Suffolk's only Honda and Suzuki dealership, has built its reputation on quality customer service for the past 25 years – but the recent growth of new competitors has meant that it has had to look to new ways of managing customer relationships

The company had developed a contact management system that included extensive details of customers and their trading history, allowing the salesforce to access records before calling customers, or to look up files when a customer called in. But it wanted to go further.

Melanie Banks, who manages the IT systems at John Banks, explains: "The contact management system was working well, but we really needed it to link to our phone system so that our sales team could see customer records even more quickly. We also wanted to make sure that customers were getting first-class service once they were on the phone. We have two sites and over 50 staff and we cannot afford to lose people in the system when they are transferred."

The solution: a new telephone system called BT Fusion, which links PCs and the telephone. "One of the immediate benefits for the sales team was the screen pop function," says Banks. "As soon as customers call in, the system recognises their number and displays their records on our PCs."

When staff aren't available, the software can be set for call forwarding and redirection to mobiles. Voicemail is stored as a file and can be forwarded to other team members. The company uses a 0800 freecall number that automatically diverts callers to the branch nearer to their home.

Banks has found that the system has made it easier to monitor the call patterns of the sales team. From her PC, she can see how active the team is – how many calls it is making and receiving.

"This may sound a bit big brother, but that's really not what it's about. It's about better use of resources. We can see when the peak times for calls are and allocate extra staff if necessary. We can even see who may need a little more help or training."

EQUIPMENT UPGRADES

Companies tend to pay less attention to their telephone equipment than they do to their computers, upgrading less often.

Upgrading to digital ISDN lines is a good first step – apart from clear voice telephony, there is a number of services that ISDN enables, such as direct dialling in (DDI) to extensions and blocks of extension numbers over a single line. Modern switchboard technology makes best use of ISDN, and best-selling systems such as Norstar and Meridian have modular upgrade paths that can add increasingly sophisticated facilities. These could include hunt groups, where calls are routed to a person who isn't engaged, and skills-based routing, where calls are routed to people best able to handle an enquiry.

Simply providing DDI numbers for staff can often end one of the most basic frustrations for outside callers – failing to reach their primary contact. Adding voicemail that can be accessed when that contact is on the move is also a good idea, as is the ability to set up call forwarding to people working at remote locations. Cordless phones in the office can also help.

Remember, however, that encouraging dependency on one individual can be a bad idea. A trap that many firms fall into is providing no backup when someone wants urgent assistance and their contact is unavailable: dialling 0 for reception often results in talking to someone with no knowledge of people's whereabouts.

OUTSOURCING

In some respects, making sure someone with the right information is available is a bigger challenge for resources-poor smaller firms than it is for their bigger counterparts. One way to give a small company a big company feel is to use facilities available directly from the operator's network. A "centrex" (as it is commonly called) means no in-house equipment is needed to implement call waiting and forwarding, conference calls and so on.

Occasional use of a specialist telesales or service organisation, during a campaign or promotion, for example, can also be a good idea. Dedicated freephone and local-rate numbers are also powerful tools for customer interaction.

It is still very much the case that many people prefer to talk to a human being – even when much routine information is available on a website or via an automated telephone response system. And, since most companies have implemented only very basic customer relationship management systems online, it is

THE NEW TECHNOLOGIES

- **The mobile extension**
  With a direct connection to a mobile operator's network, it is possible to dial mobile numbers as ordinary office extensions, adding them to the company call plan. This system is suitable for large firms with significant mobile spend. A much cheaper alternative is an option that foregoes the direct network connection but still allows mobile-to-mobile extension dialling. O_2 is offering this under the Group Worker banner.

- **The speaking directory system**
  Voice-activated directory systems reduce pressure on the switchboard. Simply by speaking a name, callers can now reach the desired individual or department without operator intervention.

- **The externally hosted company system**
  A further take on voice recognition, this picks up on the name of the person someone is trying to contact and switches the call through to a mobile, to home or to wherever they are.
  Unified messaging systems that field voice, e-mail and fax traffic for individuals or groups are also becoming popular for dispersed, mobile workforces.

still a telephone call rather than a website visit that is likely to generate the best cross-selling opportunities – particularly if it is handled by a skilled representative.

As the call centre makes way for the 'contact centre' – where staff field a range of communications with customers, partners and suppliers, including email, fax and web interactions, as well as voice, things, however, may change. (See chapter 11.)

Chapter 10

CRM rides again

After a shaky start, solutions for customer relationship management are beginning to deliver. Technology writer Marc Beishon reports

EXECUTIVE SUMMARY

■ Over-ambitious systems that are not aligned to business strategy will fall down.

■ Reliable, up-to-date information on customers can be the lifeblood of business: get a database.

■ Ask consultants, not just vendors, for advice.

■ Do not neglect sales staff as a source of customer information: they need to use the system, too.

Customer relationship management (CRM) systems have had a somewhat chequered recent history. Initial enthusiasm for them gave way to disappointment as they failed to deliver the promised benefits and showed little return on investment. The problems have been the familiar ones of major IT implementations: over-ambitious projects, unwieldy, expensive products with too much functionality, lack of clear business objectives and inattention to the vital human dimension – the views of users. But things are changing now as companies and their suppliers get wise to the real issues. In uncertain times, most CRM vendors are reporting strong interest in the UK and Europe for their solutions.

Since all firms (it is to be hoped) have customers, all have some form of CRM system – be it simply in the shape of a 'contact manager', management reporting from the accounts system, or the trusted old filing cabinet.

The key steps for starting or enhancing a CRM initiative are:

■ *Creating/upgrading the customer database to give access to clean, up-to-date data on customer contacts and histories.*

- *Prioritising the CRM project that will give most business value – and not trying to do everything at once.*

- *Choosing appropriate tools that can be implemented quickly and are not reliant on in-house resources you don't possess (such as a big IT department).*

- *Involving users fully in project development.*

- *Thinking of CRM as an ongoing process rather than a finite, 'closed' project.*

CUSTOMER DATA

Quality customer information is the bedrock of CRM. However, when business software vendor Sage conducted a survey among 1,000 UK SMEs, the results were staggering. Almost a third of respondents still rely on paper files to store information. And, a further quarter admitted to keeping no records at all. A computerised database was in use at only 37 per cent of the sample. Where records were kept, only half of the respondents knew their customers' purchase or contact histories.

Larger companies that have extensive IT resources tend to suffer from the lack of a single point of access to business information and general information overload. Few have cracked the ability to service all customer interactions at one point, especially where clients buy from several different business channels. Contact a big company by phone and this can be all too obvious: you are asked to repeat your account number as you are passed around departments; service agents do not even know the configuration of the products you've bought; there seems to be no means of tracking a shipment.

There is no question that many companies are making strenuous efforts to improve the quality of their data and, in turn, their knowledge of customers. Related to CRM systems, there is strong interest among businesses in allied types of software, including knowledge and content management tools, and business intelligence and data-mining techniques.

KEY CRM QUESTIONS

To benefit fully from a CRM solution, clarify what you want from it, by asking:

- **Strategy development:**
  - where are we and what do we want to achieve?
  - who are the customers we want and how should we segment them?

- **Value creation:**
  - how should we deliver value to our customers?
  - how should we maximise the lifetime value of the customers we want?

- **Multi-channel integration:**
  - what are the best ways for us to get to customers and for customers to get to us?
  - what does the 'perfect customer experience', deliverable at an affordable cost, look like?

- **Information management:**
  - how should we organise information on customers?
  - how can we 'replicate' the mind of the customer?

- **Performance assessment:**
  - how can we increase profits and shareholder value?
  - how should we measure our results, set standards and improve our performance?

CUSTOMER SATISFACTION

CRM, of course, is concerned with both the retention of existing customers and the attraction of new ones – with the emphasis on keeping profitable customers, both in terms of working smartly to anticipate their changing needs and in terms of the day-to-day servicing of their accounts. According to Sage's survey, SMEs see CRM coming into its own on the customer-service side – falling down on service once the customer base has reached a certain size has been a classic failing of growing firms.

Good contact handling is clearly vital when it comes to customer service – no amount of detail in the customer records will help if a caller can't reach the firm by phone, or fails to get a response by email, fax or other electronic means. Efficient contact handling is a basic tenet of CRM – but the potential is for it to be a powerful marketing tool as well as a management system. This is why CRM also stands for customer relationship marketing and why CRM systems should be driven by the marketing team, not the IT department.

KEEPING IT SIMPLE

The all-singing, all-dancing vision, however, is the downfall of many projects. So called 'point solutions' – a sales pipeline system, or a call centre where agents can see customer data – are much easier to introduce and much more likely to show returns. Electronic, self-service systems are also clear favourites for rapid return on investment: simply putting high-quality service information on a website can save many unproductive calls to agents. (It is important, however, not to give away a service that could be charged for.)

Working with a vendor-consultancy combination that's got a track record in your sector or size of project is a definite advantage. Doing a round robin of departments, asking for all the functionality that people want, then contacting vendors and sending out a 'tick list' can be a recipe for disaster: it's a '100 per cent build' before the contract is signed.

REMEMBERING THE SALESFORCE

Service and front-office customer management have been the main focus of CRM systems, but it is important not to forget the salesforce. Salespeople, especially those in a field salesforce, have tended to escape the grasp of CRM systems, which have largely been aimed at service and account management activities.

Salespeople are notorious for rejecting systems for which they see little use, and which are difficult to use. But it is vital that their up-to-date knowledge of customers is used and retained. Salesforce automation systems that both help salespeople with prospecting and direct selling, and sales managers with forecasting, can feed data back to a company about customers' needs. And if they tie into a salesperson's commission calculation, they are likely to be used.

Chapter 11

One system, many uses

Business and technology writer Marc Beishon explains what the convergence of voice and data communications means for business

EXECUTIVE SUMMARY

- The contact centre, where fax, e-mail, web and voice converge, is the future of customer service.
- The ability to carry voice traffic over the internet will cut costs and improve efficiency.
- Unified messaging will greatly increase the potential for remote working.
- Unified messaging will improve the quality of office life: you will get that fax the client sent.

The term 'convergence' has come to mean various things in the IT/ telecoms world in the past few years, but the main definitions are:

- *the convergence of data with voice calls, typically in the call centre (known as computer-telephony integration);*

- *the integration of voice and data traffic over a single company network;*

- *the bringing together of voice, email and fax in integrated inboxes – so-called unified messaging.*

THE CONTACT CENTRE

Computer telephony integration is old hat now – at least in the large and more technologically sophisticated call-handling operations. The ability to 'screen pop' – display customer information as an incoming caller is identified – is a staple application, now available to smaller firms through low-cost telephony systems that integrate with customer databases (see chapter 9).

For the state-of-the-art, you have to look to 'contact centres', which use technology that allows voice, fax, email and internet communications to be handled through one system – without the need for costly integration or desktop PC upgrades. It is forecast that 40 per cent of call centres will be upgraded to multi-channel contact centres by 2004.

Demand for the contact centre solution is being driven by a growing army of people who want to use the internet and mobile devices such as PDAs (personal digital assistants) to communicate with companies. Thanks to convergence, it is now possible to walk customers through your website or help them fill in forms online while holding a telephone conversation with at the same time.

The ability to run intelligent applications such as contact centre style systems will become even more of an imperative as customers in the business and consumer worlds become enabled with broadband internet technology. Already, more technology-savvy sectors such as computing are running help desks where customers have dual web and voice contacts with technicians.

THE SINGLE COMPANY NETWORK

For those without formal contact centre aspirations, the convergence of voice and data will nonetheless play an increasing role in day-to-day activities. This is because the 'pipe' through which all traffic, both voice and data, will arrive is an internet-style network, via the Internet Protocol (IP). The convergence of voice and data on to a single network is one of the most important current trends. The business benefits include:

- *Cost savings: routing voice traffic over an IP network saves the cost of telephony over conventional public networks. (One network is obviously cheaper to run than two – especially if it replaces some dedicated leased lines.)*

- *Simplicity: a single in-house network is easier to install and maintain.*

■ *Intelligent applications: the ability to run collaborative applications such as 'remote whiteboarding' and document sharing
and to transfer customer calls with data details.*

The combined voice/data approach is particularly good news for
companies with one or more branch offices remote from the HQ
site. Such firms often run dedicated, separate voice and data lines
between sites: with the appropriate switchboard technology, all
traffic can be diverted to the data line using 'voice over IP'.
Advantages include the elimination of an extra line, the freedom
to make multiple, simultaneous voice calls between sites at no
charge and the ability to 'break out' into the public network at
the best price – ie. staff at a firm with an HQ in London and a
remote site in Reading can make outside calls from either place
at the local rate. (See case study on page 64.)

To get this kind of system, the latest generation of IP-enabled
PBX (private branch exchange) equipment is needed at each site:
firms with several branches may choose to upgrade in stages.

It is also becoming feasible to use operators' broadband
networks to carry voice, for example, as a 'virtual private network'.
However, the take-up of this option will depend on robust service-
level agreements and delivery; most companies will prefer to run
data-only networks across public infrastructure for the time being.

UNIFIED MESSAGING

The internet is also playing a central role in the development of
unified messaging. According to analyst group Ovum, A full unified
messaging service makes:

■ *email accessible via a phone;*

■ *email accessible via a fax machine;*

■ *voicemail and fax accessible via a PC.*

The messaging mix is also being enhanced by 'instant messaging'
(a fun way of communicating messages in real time) and by the
multimedia messaging service (MMS). MMS can also handle
images and graphics.

CASE STUDY: MICHELSONS

Michelsons is a maker of neckwear, whose customers include Marks and Spencer, Next, John Lewis and Harrods. It has a head office in Sittingbourne, Kent, and a sales office in London

The company used to have a dedicated voice link between its sites that cost about £3,500 a year and allowed only one call at a time, meaning that a large number of inter-site phone calls had to be routed across the public network at an additional expense of around £300 a month.

Now, the firm runs its internal voice traffic over its data network using the Alcatel OmniPCX Office, an integrated voice, data and internet solution. This allows multiple voice calls alongside the data connection – eliminating all the previous internal-call costs – as well as voicemail to all workstations, intelligent call routing and better handset functionality so that users can tailor features to their needs.

Apart from costs savings, the main benefits are:

■ improved internal communications through the linking of telephone systems into one 'internal' switchboard;

■ improved performance from the voice and data links, giving sales staff better access to corporate data;

■ improved customer service from voicemail, call diversion and call-routing features and from provision of DDI (direct dialling in) numbers to all staff and sections.

The company's IT manager, Rob Dobell, explains: "Improved network performance has led to documents being printed across the link in remote offices rather than printed locally and faxed. Intelligent routing of calls to leave the network by the most appropriate switch, based on the destination, means that a large number of calls that were previously charged at national rates are now local calls – in particular, Sittingbourne calls to London."

Dobell adds that faxing will also be possible across the voice channels in the intersite link. "Inter-site faxing will become an internal rather than external call. And external faxing will be able to take advantage of intelligent routing."

Unified messaging is most often talked about for mobile workers who need, say, an email transcribed into speech while on the move or to have faxes appear in the email inbox. But it is also a powerful tool for office workers the ability to have those faxes channelled to the right 'desktop' rather than risk their getting 'lost' at a remote fax machine could be a great boon in the customer contact stakes. Again, it is the type of facility that is available in the latest PBX equipment.

With unified messaging comes the potential to have voicemail messages sent just like email, perhaps even to a single personal internet address, anywhere in the world, and to get them transcribed from voice to text.

CONCLUSION

Cost savings, productivity gains, increased mobility, new ways of working, better customer relationships – convergence has the power to deliver all these. Companies will need to keep a close watch on developments that suit them best.

Cut the cost of national calls by up to 55% without a 'communication access clampdown'

Reduce the cost of your company's calls with BT's Commitment Reward. You can save up to 55% on national calls and up to 28% on local calls. Plus, you could qualify for a 5% credit if you spend £500 or more on selected calls in one year. To find out more about cutting costs without causing friction in the office, **Free**fone **0800 731 3349** or connect to **BT.com/sme**

BT.com/business

Terms and conditions apply.

Connections that get results. BT

Chapter 12

Tuning in to wireless

Gary Wellburn, mobility marketing manager, Business, BT, charts the rapid advancement of mobile and wireless communications

EXECUTIVE SUMMARY

- Wireless technologies are the underpinning of the 24/7 business.

- Internet-enabled handsets allow fast data transfer and email access as well as voice services.

- GPRS allows high-speed network connections, for example, in the form of cards that are slotted into laptops.

- Wireless local area networks provide remote access to company servers and intranets.

As chapter 3 made clear, in the 24/7 society, businesses must work flexibly to meet the needs of their employees and the expectations of their customers. This chapter takes a closer look at the tools that enable flexible and 'mobile' working – wireless technologies.

WIRELESS DEVICES

Although many mobile handsets allow you to pick up your email – for example, via a connection to a laptop computer – more sophisticated devices are now on the market. GPRS handsets, 'smart phones' and PDAs (personal digital assistants) allow internet access, fast data transfer and email access as well as full voice and mobile telephone services while working on the move.

The benefits include:

- *increased efficiency;*

- *a reduction in working hours;*

■ *improved customer service – the employee can read up on a client, check stock status, or place orders with suppliers en route to the office.*

The PDA

The personal digital assistant is a hand-held computer that uses software from companies such as Palm or Microsoft to access email and diary functions and allow full synchronisation with a desk-based PC.

Blackberry

Essentially, a hand-held wireless device, Blackberry delivers emails directly to you wherever you are, allowing you to receive, read and reply to messages securely on the move. It is ideal for business people who need to be able to make quick decisions and access information and corporate email while travelling.

A Blackberry 'enterprise server' sits alongside the existing email server at the office. Once the server has been installed, flat-rate pricing means you can send and receive as much information as you need to without worrying about the ongoing costs.

The Xda

Sometimes called a 'smart phone', the Xda is becoming a byword for technological integration. A combined voice and data wireless device, it offers full-colour internet and web-based email on a PDA that also doubles as a mobile phone. It has all the functionality of a PDA, offering access to Excel, Word and all the usual applications. You can surf the net and check your emails with it as well.

The Xda enables seamless crossover between the office and remote locations – ideal for the mobile salesforce and other field workers.

WIRELESS APPLICATIONS
Mobile web

This is a piece of software that allows full internet access and email on the move – anytime, anywhere. You simply load the appropriate mobile web software on to a laptop or PDA with browser functionality and connect to a GPRS-enabled device (mobile handset or modem card). This enables you to access email and attachments, keep up-to-date with customer demands and manage business requirements, such as booking flights online.

GPRS cards

These can be slipped into the slot on most modern laptops, offering data access to the mobile web without the need for a mobile handset. They allow faster uploads and downloads of internet pages or file attachments when used in conjunction with a PDA or PC/laptop.

SMS

Short messaging service (SMS) text messages can reach a large number of customers at a fraction of the cost of traditional methods. Enterprise SMS is a software application that sits on a PC and can be used to send bulk messages to all customers or single messages to field staff/teams.

SMS can be used as a scheduling tool and a prompt for customers, allowing businesses to manage their time – and their money – more effectively. With SMS, dental practices, for example, can send simple messages to patients to remind them of their appointments, cutting the numbers of missed 'slots' and reducing downtime.

WAP

Wireless application protocol allows mobile users with wireless devices to access and interact with information and services easily. It works with hand-held digital wireless devices such as mobile phones, pagers, two-way radios and smart phones.

DATA TRANSFER SERVICES
General packet radio service

GPRS, which connects computing devices using 'packet' technology, is up to five times faster than current networks. It is only used when there is actually something to send or receive, but, like tap water, it is always on. Once logged on, you can stay online all day, transferring data when required. Charges for the service are based solely on the volume of data sent and received, not on the time spent online. The service will allow faster email access and the ability to send visual information such as maps – ideal, for example, for architects or planners on the move.

3G

The 3G (third generation) network is a convergence technology that will allow the delivery of high-quality, media-rich content including audio and video, to a mobile handset.

With 3G, you will be able to see and hear video clips, and send and receive multimedia content and information many times faster than is possible over today's current networks.

3G networks are currently being put in place by the key mobile providers and will be available for use soon.

WIRELESS NETWORKS

Wireless networks enable you to work flexibly, both in the office and on the move.

Wireless LAN is a high-speed data delivery service that supports email as well as access to existing corporate applications.

There are two types of W-LAN technology: private and public wireless LAN.

Private W-LAN

Private W-LAN technology is already used by many larger companies as a self-contained wireless office network to power communications. It can connect PCs either in a home or office environment, requiring no cabling, drilling or socket connection. Larger businesses that have wireless LAN installations will be able to extend them to employees who work flexibly from home, increasing the efficiencies of the flexible workforce and saving both money and time.

Public W-LAN

Since last July, when regulatory changes took effect, the public version of W-LAN has been commercially available in the UK. The

WIRELESS TECHNOLOGY IN ACTION

Wireless communications can be used to track vehicles and assets. A simple black box with a SIM card can be placed in any fleet vehicle

Using SMS, a vehicle can be tracked in real time, and activity reports can be generated every 20 minutes. The adoption of a wireless fleet management system could lead to a reduction in overtime claims, saving money, increasing driver efficiency and productivity, and reducing vehicle maintenance cost. According to the telematics company TOAD, an estimated £2,200 can be saved per vehicle per year.

most likely benefactors will be those who spend a significant amount of time on the move, or away from their core work area, but still need to access the company servers or intranet. The public W-LAN will provide continuous mobile/remote connection while the user is within a radius of between 100 and 500 metres of a particular access point or 'hot spot'. In this way, 'the office' will not only be transported to other sites and business premises but also to public or semi-public locations such as airports, railway stations and coffee shops.

The business user will need a W-LAN plug-in for their laptop or PDA to use the technology. With researchers from McKinsey believing that 70 per cent of all US business travellers carry laptops, the potential demand is enormous.

The speed of access is twice that of an ISDN line. Additional benefits include fast and consistent high bandwidth access while the user is stationary in public spaces, and secure remote access to corporate intranet or other internet-based services.

Chapter 13

Tomorrow's world

Graham K Whitehead, principal consultant
BTexact Technologies Foresight Consulting
Group, looks at developing ICT trends

EXECUTIVE SUMMARY

■ Greater connectivity allows for the sharing of resources between small companies.

■ New broadband technology allows data to be sent and received at the same time.

■ AORTA networks will facilitate 'anytime, any place, anywhere' access to information.

■ Artificial intelligent agents will gather data on customers and raise service levels.

Many of the office technologies we take for granted today seemed revolutionary just five or so years ago. Internet access and personalised email accounts are now so widely deployed as to be thought of as standard. But you do not have to be far into your career to remember life without them. Over the past decade, ICT has developed at an exponential rate. It will continue to do so, creating opportunities to cut business costs, improve business processes and build better relationships with customers. This chapter looks at the technology available to companies today and at how it is predicted to change over the next few years.

THE INFORMATION SUPERHIGHWAY

Since 1990, the world wide web has provided the ability for people to reach out for information. For generations to come, it will be the research tool of choice. Many school children already make the web their first source of information, and only when it fails do they resort to the encyclopedia. Every big company has a website from which information can be accessed, downloaded and printed. Web pages bring greater choice and flexibility in the way existing and potential customers interact with us – and we interact with them.

ELECTRONIC POOLING

Connection to customers is only half the story. Network connection will allow smaller companies to coalesce, sharing resources at a central location, perhaps provided by a Business Link or Chamber of Commerce.

The rationale is simple. Small businesses do not really need to have dedicated service departments. They could, for example, hand over pay-roll, tax and accounting to a local accountant who does the job not just once a month or year but in real time. Effectively, it would be like having a full-time accountant sitting in the corner ready and willing to do any task as soon as required, but only used when needed and only paid for when used. The model could equally well apply to human resources, security, health and safety, quality, web-page administration – in fact, all those activities that are essential but laborious. Technology would be deployed not only to take the headaches out of workaday tasks but also to reduce costs: the overheads, as well as the services, would be shared.

BROADBAND: THE NEXT GENERATION

As we saw in chapter 6, broadband technologies are turbocharging internet connections, cutting waiting times and costs and increasing productivity.

And this is only the beginning. BT and the broadband service provider Bulldog have recently announced the next phase of broadband development with a trial of SDSL technology. SDSL stands for symmetric digital subscriber line and, unlike ADSL, enables information to be received and sent at the same speed. It is speed that is particularly relevant to 'creative' businesses such as architectural practices and design consultancies, as it allows large volumes of documents such as computer aided design (CAD) data to be received and sent at high speed.

AORTA

However, in many ways, the acronym for the future is AORTA (Always On Real Time Access). Five years from now, it could have transformed the way we use and think about technology. We are effectively talking about the ability of machines to access information without a person being involved in the process.

In the past, it has been essential for people to know what is wanted, to know where the information is, or might be, and to know the telephone number that will connect them to the information. In the future, connection via dedicated and continuously connected pieces of wire will be low-tech. Machines will be permanently connected together and talking to each other – with humans becoming an incidental link at the end of the process.

INFORMATION HUNGER

Thanks to a 'simple' hub, most homes and businesses will become information-ready. In the future, users will not have to get the computer out, boot it, plug the wire into the phone socket, open browsers, type in the uniform resource locater (http// etc, etc.) and wait to access information. They will simply turn to their nearest display screen and ask for it. Machines will speak in a natural, human-like voice and interpret the voice sound without having to be 'trained' to understand certain vocal tones. Such instant, simple, effortless access to information will inevitably make the demand for information soar. If they are to survive and prosper in this climate, businesses will have to keep up.

ARTIFICIAL INTELLIGENCE

In addition, artificial intelligent agents will also be on hand to help complete the customer experience. These small packages of software will know people's likes and dislikes, which they will 'learn' by example. In effect, they will not need programming: they will go out across the new networks and gather information, making it instantly available on demand. This will significantly increase a business's ability to manage customers more effectively, increasing customer satisfaction and maximising revenue streams.

THE ONE-STOP SECURITY CHECK

Web-enabled services will help businesses increase the security of their networks and transactions, to streamline the processing of the buy-and-sell deal and to increase efficiency.

Imagine a credit-card check involving card, PIN number, fingerprint and visual facial recognition. Instead of having to install and maintain the functionality in the shop till, you now download the facility over the network – in real-time as the transaction is in progress. When the facility is upgraded, the new service is just downloaded automatically – no more checking if an upgrade is needed and having to install it.

The technology will not be exclusive to the retail trade: it will also be adaptable to other businesses such as exporters. Customers standing by the 'till' will be sent a message via their hand-held device and be able to see the details of the transaction. A simple press of the button, or a voice command, and value is transferred from the customer's account to the store – not from the wallet to the till drawer. All security checks have been completed: the internal chip confirms that the customer is who they say they are; the bank has been contacted to ensure that the funds are available; the credit checking agencies have agreed.

TALKING BILLBOARDS

Another development that will affect the way businesses communicate in the future is the printing circuit. This is a circuit printed on paper using processes very like those of the inkjet printer of today. If the components that can be printed emit light it will instantly be possible to make large advertising hoardings become dynamic moving pictures.

For example, an advert for a burger outlet could have a moving arrow and even dynamic information as to the current waiting times at the counter. If a small radio receiver/transmitter and aerial are printed in one corner of the hoarding, a customer could point their mobile phone at the picture and ask 'where?' They would then receive information about all outlets near their current route, including maps of how to locate them.

INTELLIGENT SHELVES, TALKING TROLLEYS

This kind of technology will transform not only advertising and promotions but also stock-taking and CRM. Consider its implications for the supermarket. The circuit could be printed inside the paper label on, say, a tin of baked beans. As the shelf stacker loads the shelf, the shelf counts the tins. As a customer removes a tin, the shelf 'knows' that one has been taken and so starts the restocking schedule. With an intelligent shelf and a little infra-red optical or wireless networking, retailers could even have dynamic shelf-edge pricing.

The possibilities do not stop there. A small interrogator in the trolley, or a network connection from the shelf to the trolley could dynamically track the customer, displaying the current contents of his or her 'shop' and the total cost as he or she moves around the store. At the checkout – without anything being lifted out of the trolley – the till would analyse the trolley contents and record the load, with maybe a secondary check on total weight, and the payment transaction would be completed.

Such tracking systems will be adapted to enhance the ability of both small and larger businesses to monitor and respond to customer needs more quickly. They will therefore be a factor in winning and sustaining competitive advantage.

In the future, demand for instant information will increase. People will want knowledge acquired and delivered in quantities that we have no concept of at present. Business transactions and exchanges of information – such as orders – will be made in real time. You will no longer need to know what connects to what and how – access to information will be seamless, effortless and ubiquitous, through technologies such as AORTA networks.

CONCLUSION

Directors need to keep their minds open to the possibilities of technology and the ways it can transform businesses for the better. They need to keep an eye on the future, while making the most of technology today.

DICTIONARY OF ICT

Marc Beishon defines some common new-tech terms

ADSL asymmetrical digital subscriber line, a technology that converts an ordinary telephone line into a high-speed internet connection.

Application service provider (ASP) a company that hosts and manages access to software applications on a subscription or rental basis.

Bandwidth the rate at which data can be transmitted over a communications network.

Broadband high-speed, permanently-on access to the internet, via services such as ADSL and cable.

CLI calling line identity, the identification of a caller's telephone number.

Contact centre a group of workers communicating with customers by the customers' chosen method voice, email, web, fax, SMS and so on.

Convergence nowadays, the merging of data and voice over a single internet-type network.

CTI computer-telephony integration, 'popping up' on screen, say, a customer's details when that customer calls in.

Data centre a facility that houses and runs computer servers.

DDI direct dialling in, to individual telephone extensions.

DECT digital enhanced cordless telecommunications, a standard for cordless handsets used at home or in the office.

DSL digital subscriber line, encompassing a family of standards that convert ordinary telephone lines into high-speed digital lines.

Enterprise resource planning (ERP) an integrated suite of business applications such as planning, manufacturing, sales, and marketing.

Extranet a private internet-style network that can embrace customers, suppliers and partners.

Firewall a system that protects company computers from intruders.

GPRS general packet radio service, the internet-style mobile network and the forerunner to third-generation mobile networks.

GSM global standard for mobile telephony, on which the current second generation mobile networks in the UK are based.

ICT information and communications technology.

Internet service provider (ISP) a company that provides home and business users with internet connectivity.

IP internet protocol, the communications 'language' that drives the internet.

Intranet an internal, private network based on internet technology

ISDN integrated digital services network, a digital telephony line that provides high speed data and high quality voice calls on a dial-up basis. ISDN also enables services such as direct dialling in (DDI) and multiple subscriber numbers on single lines.

ISP Internet service provider, offering access to the Internet as an intermediary between users and telecoms networks

Leased line a dedicated telecoms line that provides a permanent connection to an external network or data centre.

Local area network (LAN) a computer network that is usually limited to a single office or group of buildings.

Local loop the line to the local telephone exchange.

Managed service provider a company that remotely manages computer services such as security and performance applications.

Server a computer that hosts applications and data.

PBX private branch exchange, the 'switchboard' to most people, but now offered as an open computing platform that can integrate voice and data communications.

PDA personal digital assistant, handheld devices that can now combine computing power with mobile telephony

Portal a gateway to web-based services on the internet or on a company network.

SDSL symmetric digital subscriber line, a broadband business line that provides equal upstream and downstream speeds.

Self-service applications that allow customers to help themselves to information or to carry out transactions.

Service level agreement (SLA) a contract between a service provider such as an ASP and its client, describing agreed service levels, such as a guaranteed percentage of 'uptime'.

Storage service provider (SSP) a supplier that provides data storage on a remote basis.

Thin client a low-cost computer, such as a PC without a disk drive, that allows users to access applications over a network. Also called a 'network computer'.

Total cost of ownership (TCO) a way of calculating the direct and indirect costs of providing applications to users.

Unified messaging an application that provides a single point of access for services such as email, voicemail and fax.

Vertical service provider an ASP that targets certain industry sectors, such as manufacturing.

Virtual private network (VPN) a way of reserving a portion of a telecoms network for secure, private traffic.

Voice over IP voice communications over internet networks.

Wide area network (WAN) a network that links offices beyond a single location.

Wireless application service provider (WASP) a new type of ASP specialising in remote management of applications for mobile phones and laptop computers.

Wireless LAN a local area network that doesn't need physical cables to operate.

3G third generation mobile phone network, the forthcoming high-speed wireless networks that can carry multimedia traffic

USEFUL WEB SITES

Mobile computing
www.avantgo.com
www.compaq.co.uk
www.genie.co.uk
www.infosync.no
www.palm.net
www.pocketpc.com

Office equipment
www.action.com
www.apple.com
www.cisco.com
www.dell.co.uk
www.ikea.co.uk
www.inmac.co.uk
www.microsoft.com/uk
www.shareware.com

Government help/information
www.e-envoy.gov.uk
www.dti.gov.uk
www.sbs.gov.uk
www.statistics.gov.uk

Technology news
www.ananova.com
www.ntk.net
www.theregister.co.uk
www.zdnet.co.uk

Telecoms help
www.adslguide.org.uk
www.broadband-help.com
www.bt.com/business
www.oftel.com
www.telecomsadvice.org.uk

Customer relationship management
www.crm-forum.com
www.1to1.com